STUDYING
RHYTHM

STUDYING RHYTHM

Anne Carothers Hall

Wilfrid Laurier University

PRENTICE HALL, Englewood Cliffs, New Jersey 07632

Library of Congress Cataloging-in-Publication Data

HALL, ANNE CAROTHERS (date)
   Studying rhythm.

   1. Musical meter and rhythm—Studies and exercises.
I. Title.
MT42.H28 1989   88–23418
ISBN 0–13–855651–2

Editorial/production supervision
   and interior design: F. Hubert
Cover design: Baldino Design
Manufacturing buyer: Ray Keating

Printed in the United States of America

10   9   8   7   6   5

0-13-855651-2

PRENTICE-HALL INTERNATIONAL (UK) LIMITED, *London*
PRENTICE-HALL OF AUSTRALIA PTY. LIMITED, *Sydney*
PRENTICE-HALL CANADA INC., *Toronto*
PRENTICE-HALL HISPANOAMERICANA, S.A., *Mexico*
PRENTICE-HALL OF INDIA PRIVATE LIMITED, *New Delhi*
PRENTICE-HALL OF JAPAN, INC., *Tokyo*
SIMON & SCHUSTER ASIA PTE. LTD., *Singapore*
EDITORA PRENTICE-HALL DO BRASIL, LTDA., *Rio de Janeiro*

This book is dedicated to
Wallace Berry

CONTENTS

STUDYING
RHYTHM

INTRODUCTION

This book contains extended rhythmic studies and preparatory exercises. They are intended to be sung, spoken, and tapped or clapped. Singing is best because, unlike speaking, it promotes the conviction that we are engaged in a musical activity, and, unlike clapping, it allows us to give the notes their full durations, rather than simply perform the attack pattern. Also, unlike clapping, singing leaves the hands free to conduct the meter. We need not sing all the notes on one pitch; making up tunes to fit the rhythmic patterns and mood can be entertaining. In group performance, as in class, singing the various notes of a triad is another option. In spite of this strong recommendation to sing the studies, clapping may be the best way to check the accuracy of an ensemble performance. And tapping or clapping and counting aloud may be a good way to begin learning a study. In addition, tapping or clapping is necessary for solo performance of the two-part studies, as explained below.

Studies may be sung on any simple syllable that begins with a good definite consonant; "ta" is obvious. For very fast patterns, it is much easier to alternate syllables: ta-fa-te-fe is easier to sing rapidly than ta-ta-ta-ta. We should also remember that lightness facilitates speed; in approaching a fast passage, anxiety may make us tense so that we sing louder or clap harder, making the passage more difficult. It is well to believe that fast means soft.

The studies are identified by letters following the chapter number (1.A, 3.C). They are composed of well-defined phrases grouped in simple musical forms: statement, contrast, and return, or statement and variations. The studies are meant to be *studied*, not just sight-read. Many of them are quite long, and many of them will challenge even experienced musicians. There is no point in studying them unless they are worked to a level of good performance. Rhythm is either right, or it is a different rhythm. Unless two against three is an exactly even two against an exactly even three, the whole point of the pattern is lost. When we strive for real precision, even the simplest rhythm may serve as a valuable study in ensemble. It is surprisingly difficult for fifteen people to clap at exactly the same time.

The two-part studies may be performed with one or more people on each part. They are designed, however, for solo performance, with the upper part sung and the lower part tapped or clapped. This method requires the performer to hear both parts independently in a way that tapping both parts does not. Most musicians will find the two-part studies much more difficult than the single lines. Since so much of our music is composed of lines with their own integrity, working to develop the ability to think two lines at once is well worth the considerable effort it may require.

The exercises, identified by numbers following the chapter number (1.1, 3.2), serve as preparation for the studies that they precede. They consist of single measures, or pairs of measures, separated by whole-measure rests. Metronome markings for an exercise suggest a range of tempi possible for the performance of all its segments, but individual segments may be performed faster. Each segment of an exercise should be repeated several times, until it is easy, before continuing to the next segment. The ability to repeat a pattern is evidence that we can perform it. If we can perform a pattern once, but not three or four times in succession, then we have not really conquered it. Spending enough time on a segment to memorize it is a good way to ensure that the rhythmic pattern has been completely grasped. The exercises are not necessarily complete preparation for the studies; rather, they serve as models. Where individual patterns in the studies seem difficult, they should be extracted and practiced.

In performing the studies, the goal must always be to grasp the rhythm of the phrase as a whole. Reading music note-by-note is as useless as reading prose letter-by-letter. Reading a beat at a time is like reading a word at a time, and the lack of comprehension will be audible whether the performer is reading music or poetry. A musical phrase, a musical gesture, must be comprehended as a whole. To break a phrase, by hesitation or by reiteration of a fragment, is to destroy it. We must arrive at cadences on time; in ensemble performance, arriving late is embarrassing, to say the least. So while we should aim for absolute accuracy, we miss the point if we concentrate on the details at the expense of the shape of the long phrase. The phrase must be understood as a continuous flow, articulated and enlivened by the patterns within it.

If sustaining the phrase is important, so is breathing between phrases. Usually there are notated rests between phrases. Occasionally, however, only a comma or phrase mark indicates where the performer must sneak a breath without significantly delaying the beat. An unbroken flow of sound, like too many run-on sentences, makes both performer and listener physically uncomfortable—out of breath. Breathing is vital.

In all the studies, the notes must be given their full durations (except when we snatch a breath between phrases). Accurate performance does not allow us to begin a silence too soon, or to add a silence, any more than it allows us to begin a sound too soon, or to add a sound. Because we tend to concentrate on *beginning* each note correctly, we often find it difficult to listen to the full duration of each sound, to pay attention to its continuation and ending. However, in order to project a line, we must hear the whole of every sound. (Again, this is why singing the studies is better than clapping them.)

The tempo indications given for the studies should be observed. We may practice an Allegro study slowly, but we should be able to perform each study at the given tempo. We do, after all, have to perform both slow music and fast music. Nothing will make the studies more boring than working on them all at the same moderate tempo. (Neither coffee nor lemonade tastes best lukewarm.)

Metronomes are not to be scorned as a means of checking steadiness of tempo. Metronome indications for precise tempi have been given for all the studies. They are suggestions only, and in some cases may not be appropriate for the level of skill of a student. In general, however, we should consider a study learned only when we can perform it with a metronome at a tempo close to the one indicated. On the other hand, too much practice with a metronome may foster dependence on it. We must learn to keep a steady beat without such mechanical help. And musical rhythm is not as unrelentingly steady as a metronome, so metronomic regularity cannot be our ultimate goal.

Metronome numbers indicate the number of ticks per minute. Thus, longer values are represented by lower numbers. (In a given tempo there are fewer half-notes than eighth-notes per minute.) This principle must be understood in order to figure out equivalences. If the eighth-note is constant at 108, for example, then the sixteenth-note, half as long, is at 216, and the quarter-note is at 54; the dotted-quarter, three times as long as an eighth, is a third as fast at 36.

Conducting the meter both helps keep the beat steady and lets the hand take care of counting beats. We should conduct while singing the one-part exercises and studies, so that conducting becomes natural. Only when we can perform the beat patterns without thinking about them does conducting become a help. If beating time seems a hindrance rather than a help—one more thing to think about—then it should be practiced assiduously, for it is an essential tool for musicians. However, we must not grow dependent on our hands to keep the beat because they will, in many musical situations, be otherwise occupied. We should therefore also practice the studies without conducting.

Because the studies are composed of phrases, they are suitable for dictation. The greatest benefit of dictation, once we know how to write the small patterns, is the development of memory. Therefore, one person should sing a phrase until those taking dictation can sing it back; only then should they write it. Individuals working alone can develop skill by reading a phrase until it is memorized, then writing it.

While the chapters are arranged to form a logical progression, and within the chapters the studies are arranged in order of increasing difficulty, it is not necessary to learn all the studies in one chapter before proceeding to the next. To work straight through the book may not be as helpful as to do some of the studies in each chapter and then to return to earlier chapters and work some of the other studies. Performance of complicated rhythmic patterns, changing meters, unequal beats, and cross-rhythms is not learned once and then known forever, any more than is performance of scales; we have to keep practicing.

Understanding the basic processes of musical rhythm is necessary for good musical performance. Musical rhythm is complex and difficult to describe because of the number of factors involved and their interdependence.[1] Rhythm is made by durations of sound and silence and by accent. Accent is made by many factors, of which loudness, making a stress accent, is just one. Duration makes accent, as a longer note is emphasized by its length, so these two basic factors of rhythm are not separable.[2]

The rhythm in this book, like the rhythm of most Western art music, is metrical. Meter is the grouping by accent of normally regular pulses (beats) into measures beginning with stronger accents. Within the measure, there is a hierarchy of beats and parts of beats, in that some beats are stronger than others, and beats are stronger than half-beats, which are in turn stronger than quarter-beats, etc. When rhythm is metrical, the rhythmic patterns are heard against a background of regularly recurring pulses and accents. When accents of stress and duration do not coincide with metrical accents, the result is syncopation.

Just as one factor of rhythmic pattern, duration, can produce the other factor, accent, rhythmic patterns produce the meter they are heard against. That is, meter is made audible through sounding rhythmic patterns; only after the meter is established will the listener retain it as a set of expectations and hear a rhythmic pattern agree or conflict with it. Much of the fun of metrical rhythm, and its expressive power, derive from the interplay of irregular patterns and metrical regularity, and the performer should enjoy this interplay and project it for the audience to enjoy.

It is common in performance to stress the downbeat slightly. The stress seems especially necessary in unpitched performance. (In much music, the downbeat accent is made by harmonic change, and no additional stress is necessary or desirable.) However, once the meter is established, then the listener hears a metrical accent on the downbeat, and the performer must consider the musical context to determine how much stress accent, if any, should be added to the metrical accent. Long notes have their own accents, and additional stress accent may make a note too conspicuous. Too much accent breaks a musical line into pieces. We must be sensitive to accent if our performance is to be musical.

We speak of musical rhythm as composed of various discrete units: beats, measures, patterns of different lengths. But the essential quality of musical rhythm is ongoingness.[3] Most downbeats function both as goal of the preceding measure and as beginning of the new one. Patterns articulate a continuous flow. For rhythm to function as music, it must have this flow. We must, while aiming for a correct performance of rhythmic patterns, strive always to create the articulated flow of musical rhythm.

Notes

[1] For an extended discussion of the complexity of rhythm, see Wallace Berry, *Structural Functions in Music* (Englewood Cliffs, NJ: Prentice Hall, 1976), pp. 301-424. For an extensive bibliography, see Jonathan D. Kramer, "Studies of Time and Music: A Bibliography," *Music Theory Spectrum*, 7 (1985): 72-106.

[2] The accent a note has by virtue of being longer than the surrounding notes is often called an "agogic" accent, although this is not the term's original meaning. See the explanation of "agogic" in the *Harvard Dictionary of Music*.

³ *Cf.* Susanne Langer's assertion that the essential characteristic of any rhythmic motion is that the end of one action is the beginning of the next, in *Problems of Art* (New York: Charles Scribner's Sons, 1957), pp. 50-51.

1. TWO-FOUR METER

This chapter is devoted to two-four time, with no notes shorter than eighth-notes. The relatively simple material allows us to concentrate on the techniques of performing the rhythmic studies: conducting the meter while singing the rhythm, improvising melodies with the given rhythm, performing in time with a metronome, and singing one rhythm while clapping another.

Conducting duple meter is rather like bouncing an imaginary ball, with the point of the beat at the point of contact with the ball. On the downbeat, the right hand descends and rebounds away from the body, tracing a backwards J; on the upbeat, the hand traces the same figure in reverse.

We should be aware of the structure of the two-part studies. Study 1.I is the first of many canons; here, the clapped part leads the sung part by one beat. Study 1.H is the first of many where one part is an ostinato.

The notation of rests is often governed by different rules from the notation of notes. A note lasting a whole measure in two-four is a half-note, but a rest lasting a whole measure is a whole rest, as in three-four and four-four and other meters.

1. 1) ♩ = 60 - 160

1. A)   Allegro (♩ = 144)

1. B)   Allegretto (♩ = 120)

1. C)   Presto (♩ = 168)

1. 2)   ♩ = 66 - 160

1. D)   Vivo (♩ = 144)

1. E)   Allegretto (♩ = 100)

1. 3)   ♩ = 60 - 160

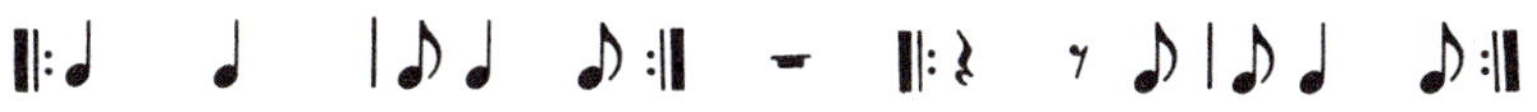

1. F) Andante (♩= 88)

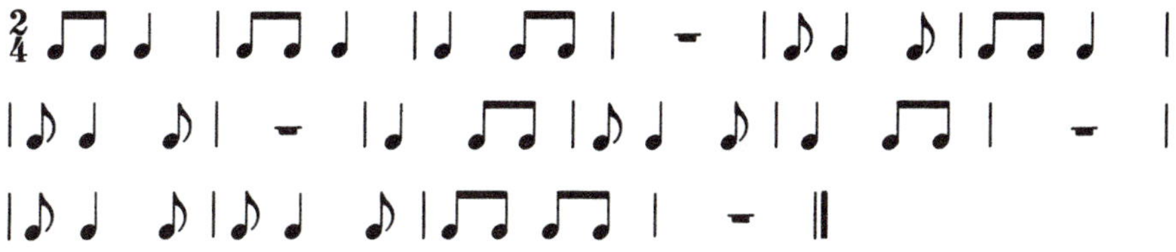

1. G) Allegretto (♩= 108)

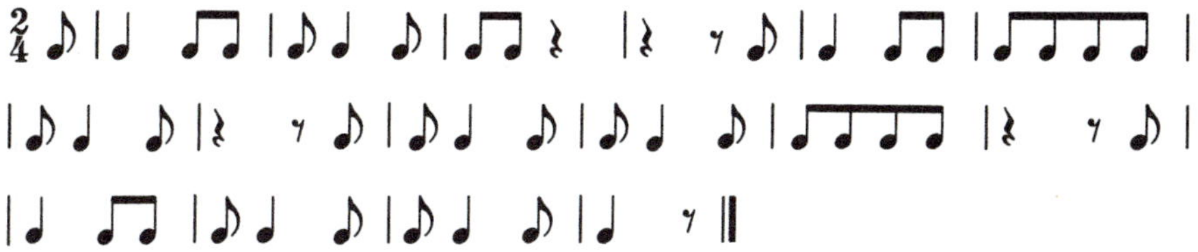

1. 4) ♩= 72 - 144

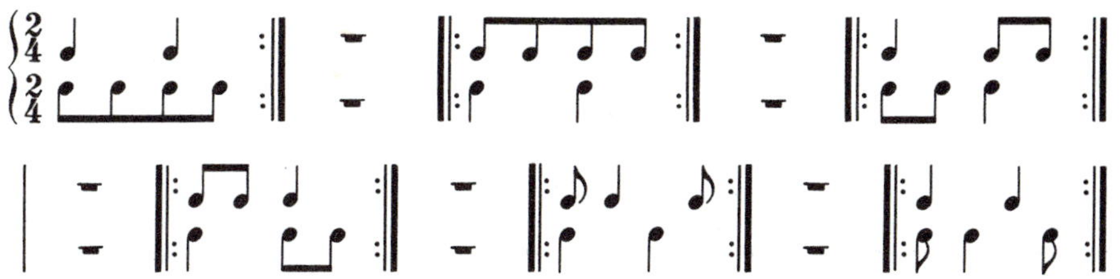

1. H) Moderato (♩= 100)

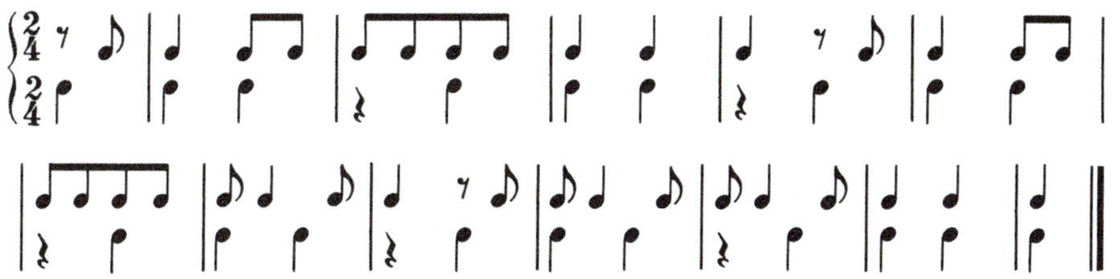

1. I)   Allegro (♩ = 132)

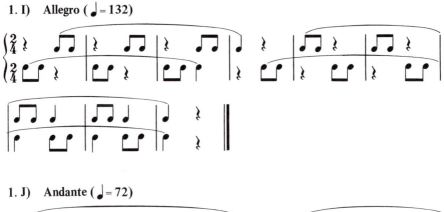

1. J)   Andante (♩ = 72)

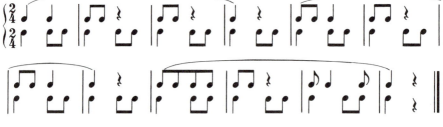

1. K)   Allegro (♩ = 100)

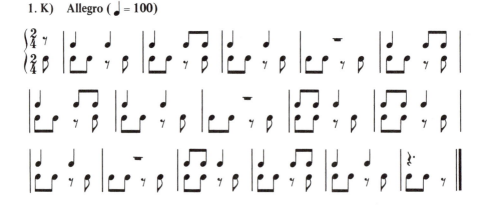

1. L)   Presto (♩ = 132)

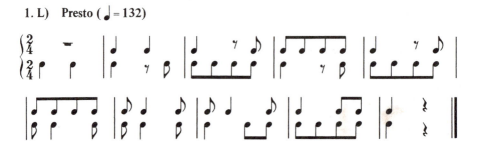

2. THREE-FOUR METER

Three-four meter is more complex than two-four not only because it has another beat, but because, although the downbeat remains strongest, the relative strengths of the second and third beats may shift. In conducting, the right hand hooks slightly to the left on the downbeat in order to move out to the right on the second beat and diagonally back up to the starting point on the third beat.

Although half-notes are used for two beats in three-four meter, half rests are not used in this meter. Two beats of silence require two quarter rests.

2. 2) ♩ = 60 - 160

2. D)   Allegro (♩ = 152)

2. E)   Andante (♩ = 96)

2. 3) ♩ = 60 - 160

2. F)   Allegretto (♩ = 112)

2. G)   Allegro (♩ = 138)

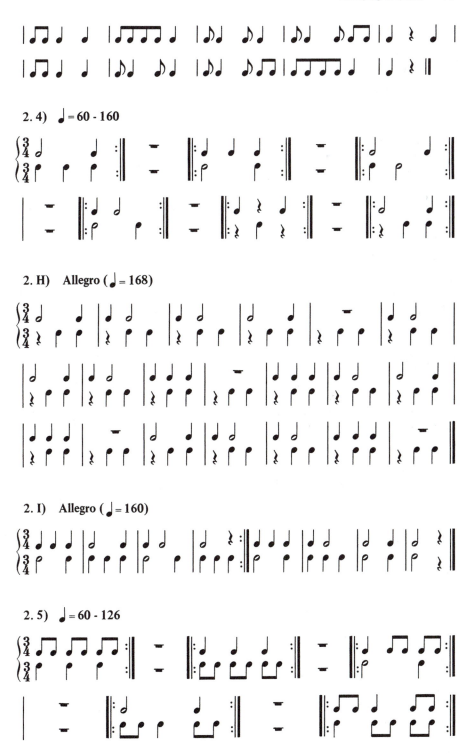

2. 4) ♩ = 60 - 160

2. H)   Allegro (♩ = 168)

2. I)   Allegro (♩ = 160)

2. 5) ♩ = 60 - 126

2. J)   Allegretto (♩ = 100)

2. K)   Allegro (♩ = 120)

2. L)   Vivace (♩ = 138)

3. FOUR-FOUR METER

In some compositions in four-four meter, the first and third quarters are clearly the main strong and weak beats, like the two quarters in two-four. Other times, the four-four measure is more like two two-four measures, and the first and third beats are about equally strong.

In conducting four, the right hand hooks slightly to the right on the down-beat, so it can move left on the second beat. On the third beat, which is the second strong beat, the hand moves out to the right, and on the last beat, as always, it returns up to the starting point.

In Study 3.E, as in comparable situations, the stress marks indicate just enough impulse to make the downbeat clear when the second beat is accented by a longer note.

3. 1) ♩ = 76 - 176

3. A)   Allegretto (♩ = 108)

D M   S F M   R D R   D   D F M F S D A

S M F   R   M F S L T D   D M D F

S F M   F M   R   D M S M   D

3. B)   Allegro (♩ = 120)

3. C)   Vivace (♩ = 144)

3. 2) ♩ = 60 - 160

3. D)   Andante (♩ = 80)

3. E)   Presto (♩ = 160)

3. F)   Allegro moderato (♩ = 120)

3. 3)   ♩ = 66 - 168

3. G)   Allegretto (♩ = 100)

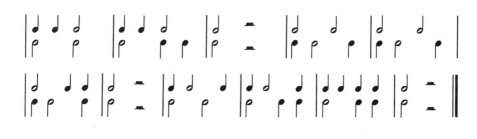

3. H)   Vivace (♩ = 144)

3. 4)   ♩ = 60 - 120

3. I)   Vivo (♩ = 144)

3. J)   Allegretto (♩ = 88)

3. K)   Allegro (♩ = 108)

4. DOTTED QUARTERS AND TIED EIGHTHS IN SIMPLE METER

A dot extends a note by half the value of the note, so a dotted quarter-note represents a quarter extended by an eighth-note:

Dots must be used instead of ties whenever possible. However, it is a rule of notation that only a whole note, a dotted half-note, or a half-note beginning on the second beat may span the middle of a four-four measure. Therefore, a tie must be used when the value of a dotted quarter spans the middle of a four-four measure, as in the third and fourth measures below:

In performing dotted and tied notes, conducting will help us feel the beat, and so help us place correctly a note that follows off the beat.

4. 1) ♩ = 72 - 144

4. A)   Andante con moto (♩ = 92)

4. B)   Allegro (♩ = 120)

4. C)   Allegro (♩ = 132)

4. 2)   ♩ = 72 - 144

4. D)   Allegretto (♩ = 100)

4. E)   Allegro (♩ = 120)

4. F)   Allegro (♩ = 126)

4. 3)   ♩ = 60 - 120

4. G)   Andante (♩ = 84)

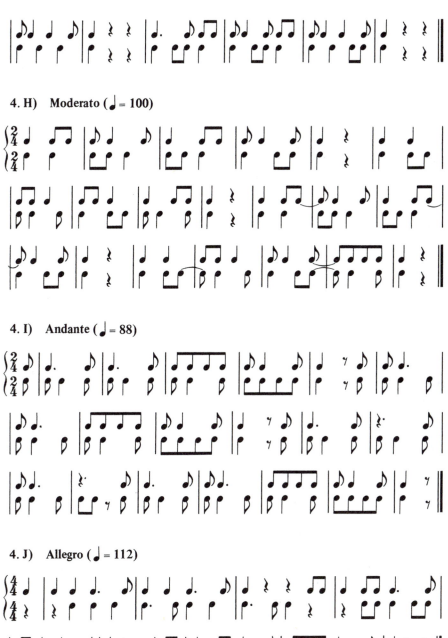

4. H)   Moderato (♩ = 100)

4. I)   Andante (♩ = 88)

4. J)   Allegro (♩ = 112)

5. SIX-EIGHT METER

In six-eight, as in all compound meters, the basic division of the beat is by three. Thus, six-eight is a duple meter, with two beats to the measure, and the dotted-quarter beat is basically divided into three eighth-notes. It is important to realize the lack of similarity between the signatures of simple and compound meters. Two-four means two quarter-note beats in a measure, whereas six-eight means two dotted-quarter beats in a measure. Except in very slow tempi, six-eight should be conducted in two, so the triple division of the compound beat is felt. This is why tempi are given for the dotted quarter rather than the eighth-note.

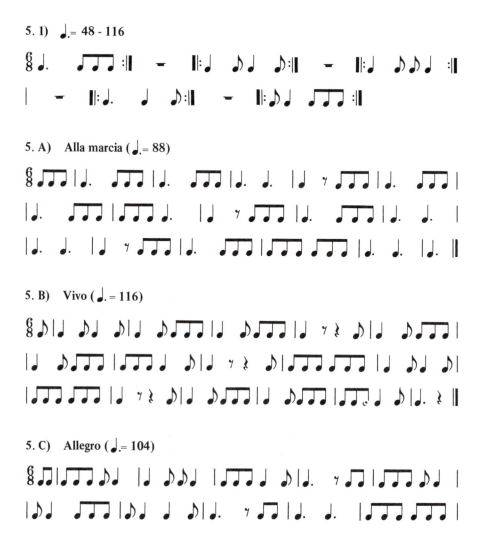

5. 1)   ♩.= 48 - 116

5. A)   Alla marcia (♩.= 88)

5. B)   Vivo (♩. = 116)

5. C)   Allegro (♩.= 104)

5. D)   Vivace (♩. = 120)

5. E)   Allegretto (♩. = 84)

5. F)   Presto (♩. = 126)

5. 2)   ♩.= 48 - 100

5. G)   Allegretto (♩. = 88)

5. H)   Andante (♩.= 69)

5. I)   Allegretto (♩.= 84)

5. J)   Andante ($\boldsymbol{\cdot}$ = 66)

6. SIXTEENTH-NOTES IN SIMPLE METER

In learning sixteenth-note patterns, speaking the names of the notes in rhythm reinforces the correlation between the sound of patterns and their notation:

eight   sixteen   sixteen   eight   six   eight   teen   sixteen   sixteen

"Eight" and "sixteen" are easier to repeat rapidly than "eighth" and "sixteenth." "Six" names the first or accented of two sixteenth-notes, "teen" names the second, unaccented one. This system also works for quarters and dotted quarters, although the single notes must be spoken in two or three syllables as even eighth-notes:

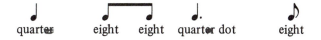

quarter   eight   eight   quarter dot   eight

This approach to rhythm deals entirely with sound rather than with numbers. It is, incidentally, excellent for teaching rhythm to youngsters who do not like the arithmetic involved in counting.

6. 1)   ♩ = 48 - 100

6. A)   Andante (♩ = 52)

6. B)   Allegro (♩ = 96)

6. C)   Allegro ma non troppo, leggiero (♩ = 84)

6. D)   Andante (♩ = 72)

6. E)   Allegretto (♩ = 76)

6. F)   Presto (♩ = 108)

6. 2)   ♩ = 40 - 80

6. G)   Adagio (♩ = 52)

6. H)   Andante (♩ = 60)

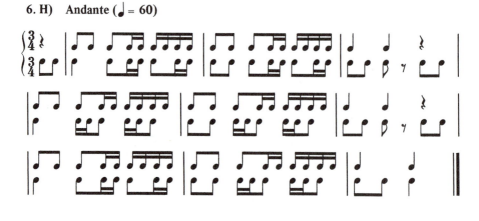

6. I)   Allegretto (♩ = 72)

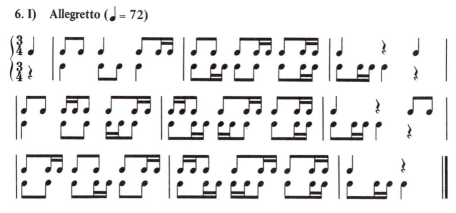

6. J)   Allegro non troppo (♩ = 76)

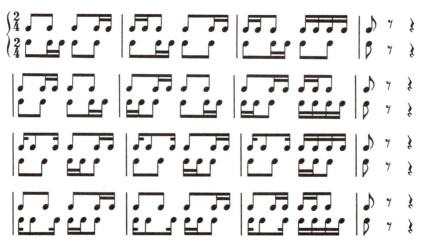

7. DOTTED EIGHTHS IN SIMPLE METER

Since a dot adds to a note half of its value, a dot adds to an eighth-note the value of a sixteenth-note:

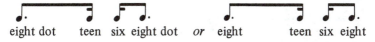

In speaking these patterns in the manner explained at the beginning of Chapter 6, the dot may be spoken or the syllable "eight" may be given its extra length: saying "dot" reminds us of the notation, while just extending "eight" allows us to speak the pattern in its rhythm:

eight dot   teen six eight dot   *or*   eight   teen six eight

The double dot, introduced in Study 7. C, adds to a note three quarters of its value (half plus half of the half); the double dot thus almost doubles the value of a note:

7. 1)   ♩ = 52 - 100

7. A)   Allegretto (♩ = 72)

7. B)   Allegro (♩ = 100)

7. C)   Andante con moto (♩ = 63)

7. D)   Allegro ma non troppo (♩ = 104)

7. E)   Allegretto (♩ = 80)

7. F)   Allegro maestoso (♩ = 92)

7. 2) ♩ = 48 - 84

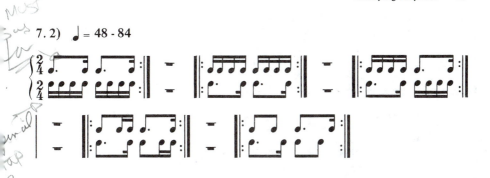

7. G)   Andante (♩ = 69)

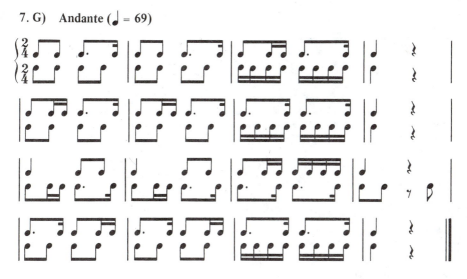

7. H)   Andante (♩ = 66)

7. 3) ♩ = 48 - 84

7. I)   Andante (♩ = 66)

7. J)   Allegretto (♩ = 76)

8. SIXTEENTH-NOTES IN SIX-EIGHT METER

There are twenty-four possible patterns made of sixteenth-notes, eighth-notes, and dotted eighths that will constitute a dotted-quarter beat in compound time. Performing the patterns by speaking the note-values in rhythm is a good way to become familiar with them:

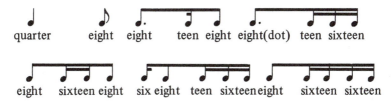

quarter   eight eight   teen eight eight(dot)   teen sixteen

eight   sixteen eight   six eight   teen sixteen eight   sixteen sixteen

The convention of notation that sixteenth-notes within a beat be beamed together makes it difficult in some patterns to see the basic three eighth-notes of the dotted-quarter beat. ♩. ♬ has to be understood as ♩. ♬♪, for example.

In Exercise 8.2, voice and hands reverse parts within each measure. Therefore, the single beats should be practiced until they can be performed easily; only then should whole measures be attempted.

8. 1) ♩. = 40 - 76

8. A)   Grazioso (♩. = 66)

8. B)   Adagio ($\sheetnote$. = 52)

8. C)   Allegro ($\sheetnote$. = 88)

8. D)   Allegretto ($\sheetnote$. = 66)

8. E)   Allegro ($\sheetnote$. = 80)

8. F)   Andante ($\flat$. = 60)

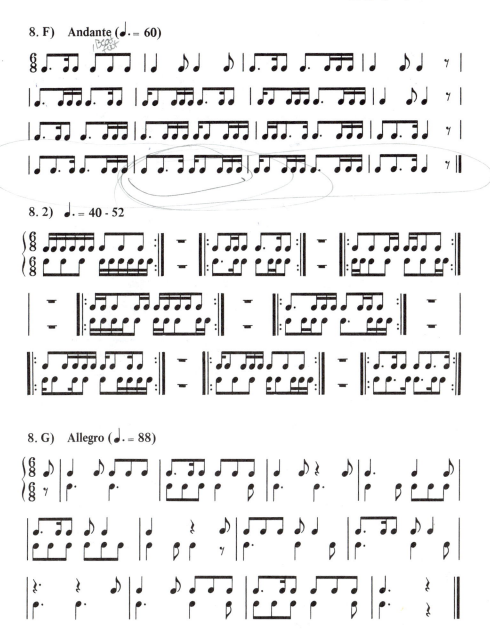

8. 2) $\flat$. = 40 - 52

8. G)   Allegro ($\flat$. = 88)

8. H) Allegretto (♩. = 56)

8. I) Andante (♩. = 48)

8. J) Adagio (♩. = 44)

9. MORE RESTS AND SYNCOPATION IN SIMPLE METER

In performing studies with syncopated patterns involving sixteenth-notes, it may be helpful to tap the eighth-note divisions of the beat or to use a metronome set at the tempo of the eighth-note. In studies with frequent rests, we should still aim to understand and project whole phrases. Rests interrupt the sound, but they should not interrupt the flow of the phrase.

9. 1) ♩ = 56 - 96

9. A) Allegretto (♩ = 88)

9. B) Vivace (♩ = 132)

9. C) Moderato (♩ = 84)

9. D)   Allegretto ($\downarrow = 80$)

9. E)   Allegro ($\downarrow = 96$)

9. F)   Allegretto ($\downarrow = 72$)

9. 2) $\downarrow = 40 - 60$

9. G)   Allegretto (♩ = 100)

9. H)   Moderato (♩ = 69)

9. I)   Allegro (♩ = 92)

9. J)   Allegretto (♩ = 72)

10. MORE RESTS AND SYNCOPATION
IN SIX-EIGHT METER

Because the beats are longer in six-eight than in simple meter, tapping the eighth-note or using a metronome set at the speed of the eighth, until the patterns are thoroughly familiar, may be even more important in ensuring correct performance.

10. 1) ♩. = 40 - 72

10. A)   Vivace (♩. = 112)

10. B)   Vivo (♩. = 108)

10. C)   Andante (♩. = 52)

10. D)   Allegretto (♩. = 66)

10. E)   Allegro (♩. = 72)

10. F)   Adagio (♩. = 40)

10. 2)   ♩. = 40 - 60

10. G)   Allegretto (♩. = 56)

10. H)   Andante (♩. = 48)

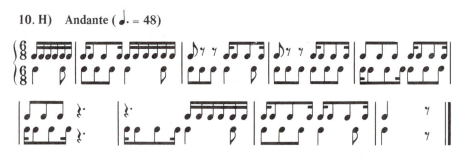

10. I)   Moderato (♩. = 56)

10. J)   Allegro (♩. = 63)

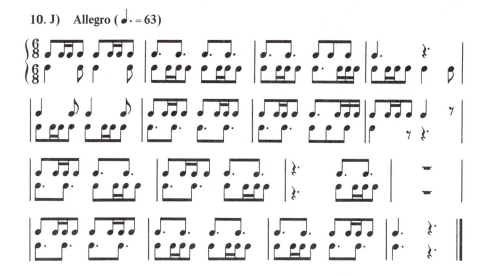

11. NINE-EIGHT AND TWELVE-EIGHT METER

Nine-eight and twelve-eight meter combine the compound beat patterns of six-eight with the three and four beats of three-four and four-four meter; hence, there are no new problems here. In Exercise 11.3 especially, single beats should be repeated until they seem easy before whole measures are attempted.

11. 1)   ♩. = 40 - 66

11. A)   Allegro vivo (♩. = 120)

11. B) Con moto ($\downarrow. = 60$)

11. C) Allegretto ($\downarrow. = 63$)

11. 2) $\downarrow. = 56 - 76$

11. D) Allegro maestoso ($\downarrow. = 104$)

11. E) Andante con moto ($\downarrow. = 66$)

(3)

11. F)   Andante (♩. = 56)

11. 3)   ♩. = 40 - 60

11. G)   Allegro non troppo (♩. = 88)

11. H)   Andante (♩. = 56)

11. I)   Allegretto (♩. = 60)

Fine

Da capo al fine

11. J)   Adagio (♩. = 48)

12. TRIPLETS

The division of the beat into thirds is familiar from compound meter. The new problem here is performing in succession duple and triple divisions of the beat. A common tendency, when moving from duplet to triplet eighth-notes, is to make the first note of a triplet too long. It may help to realize that a third of a beat is closer in length to a quarter of a beat than to half of a beat, so triplet eighths are more like sixteenth-notes than they are like eighth-notes. When beginning a triplet, we must move quickly to its second note, rather than sit on the first note. When alternating different divisions of the beat, it is helpful to use a metronome enough to ensure that the beat stays constant.

Successions of eighths, triplets, and sixteenths may be performed by numbering aloud the notes on each beat:

12. 1)   ♩ = 60 - 100

12. A)   Allegro ma non troppo (♩ = 112)

12. B)   Moderato (♩ = 88)

12. C)   Andante (♩ = 66)

Conductir 3

12. D)   Allegro (♩ = 100)

12. E)   Andante con moto (♩ = 76)

12. F)   Allegretto (♩ = 92)

12. 2) ♩ = 48 - 84

12. G)   Andante (♩ = 80)

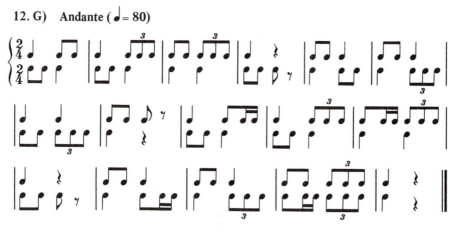

12. H)   Andante (♩ = 80)

12. I)   Con moto (♩ = 72)

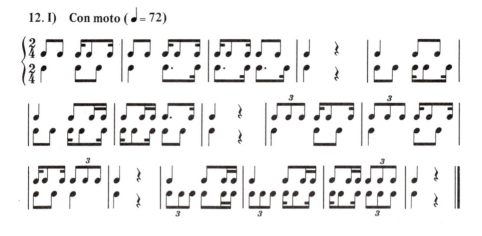

12. J)   Allegro ma non troppo (♩. = 112)

13. TWO AGAINST THREE

We have already encountered two against three in Chapter 10, in the division of the dotted-quarter beat of six-eight meter into two dotted eighth-notes that we hear against the basic triple division of the beat.

The performance of cross-rhythms requires understanding the numerical relations involved. When two eighths sound against triplet eighths, each of the duplet eighths is three sixths of a beat, so the duplet eighths begin on the first and fourth sixths of the beat; each of the triplet eighths is two sixths of a beat, so they begin on the first, third, and fifth sixths of the beat. Grasping the composite patterns may be facilitated by speaking verbal phrases that we naturally speak in these rhythms:

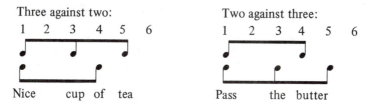

It is relatively easy to hear and perform the composite pattern made by two against three, as the rhythm of the pattern — ♪♫ — is familiar. However, it is musically important to be able to hear the duplet and triplet as independent concurrent patterns. For this reason, we need to practice two against three slowly so as to hear that the composite pattern is correct *and* quickly so that we can hear two and three at the same time but independent of each other.

13. 1) ♩. = 40 - 69

13. A)   Allegretto (♩. = 52)

13. B)   Allegro (♩ = 66)

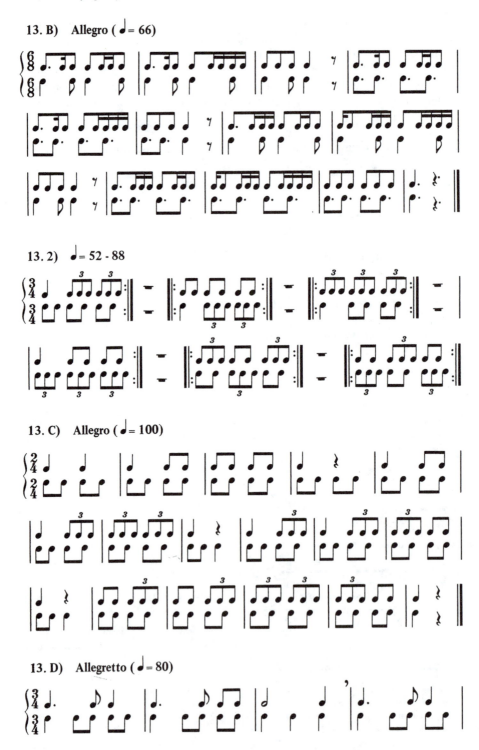

13. 2)   ♩ = 52 - 88

13. C)   Allegro (♩ = 100)

13. D)   Allegretto (♩ = 80)

13. 3) ♩ = 48 - 96

13. E)   Allegro ma non troppo (♩ = 96)

13. F)   Andante (♩ = 69)

13. G)   Andantino ($\frac{3}{4}$ ♩ = $\frac{9}{8}$ ♩. = 69)

13. H)   Allegretto (♩ = 84)

13. 4) ♩ = 50 - 80

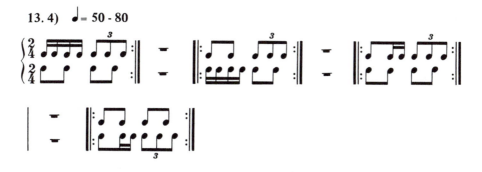

13. I)   Allegretto (♩ = 88)

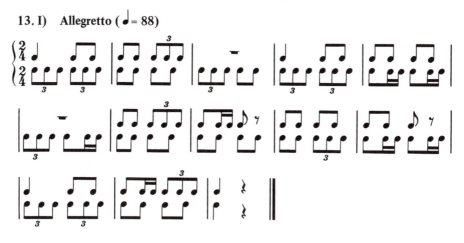

13. J)   Adagio (♩ = 52)

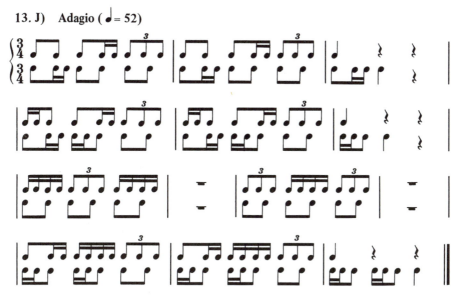

14. HALF-NOTE BEAT

When no values smaller than eighth-notes are involved, the half-note beat presents no new rhythmic difficulties, but simply a reading problem: We must *see* a half-note as one beat instead of two, and see a whole note as only two beats, and a quarter-note as half a beat. Sixteenth-notes divide the beat into eight parts.

The new symbol in this chapter is the breve, which equals two whole notes (see the first measure of study 14. H). The whole rest continues to be used for a whole measure rest, even though it is also used for a half-measure rest in four-two time. The whole rest is not used for two beats in three-two time, just as the half rest is not used for two beats in three-four time.

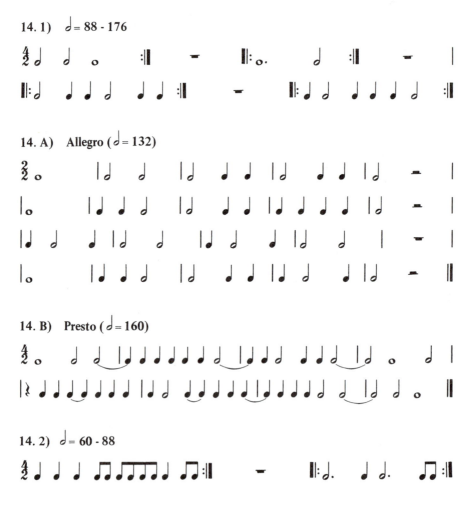

14. 1) ♩ = 88 - 176

14. A) Allegro (♩ = 132)

14. B) Presto (♩ = 160)

14. 2) ♩ = 60 - 88

14. C)   Vivace (♩ = 120)

14. D)   Allegretto (♩ = 92)

14. 3)   ♩ = 48 - 60

14. E)   Adagio (♩ = 60)

14. F)   Largo (♩ = 44)

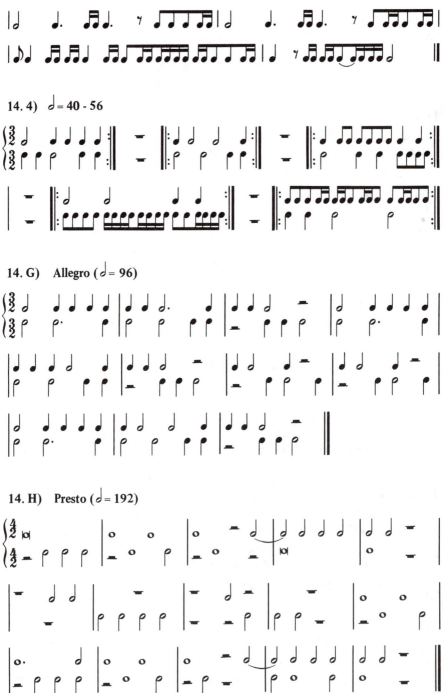

14. I)   Allegro ma non troppo ($\flat$ = 104)

14. J)   Adagio ($\flat$ = 40)

15. DOTTED-HALF-NOTE BEAT

Reading six-four and nine-four meter, we quickly learn to appreciate the clarity with which beams show beats in six-eight and nine-eight meter. Here, we have to learn to see nine consecutive quarter-notes as constituting three beats.

15. 1) $\flat \cdot$ = 48 - 72

15. A)   Allegro (♩. = 108)

15. B)   Adagio (♩. = 56)

15. C)   Vivace (♩. = 126)

15. D)   Andante (♩. = 60)

15. E)   Allegro (♩. = 72)

15. F)   Allegro (♩. = 116)

15. 2)   ♩. = 40 - 60

15. G)   Andante (♩. = 60)

15. H)   Moderato (♩. = 72)

15. I)   Allegretto (♩. = 52)

15. J)   Andante (♩. = 44)

16. EIGHTH-NOTE BEAT

There are no new rhythmic problems here, but simply the problem of seeing an eighth-note as equal to a beat, a quarter-note as equal to two beats, a thirty-second-note as equal to a quarter of a beat.

The four syllables of "thirty-second" may be spoken evenly so as to match the four thirty-second notes within the time of an eighth-note. Although the syllables become too tricky to be useful in some dotted and syncopated patterns, speaking the names of the note-values may be helpful in learning the more straight-forward patterns of eighths, sixteenths, and thirty-seconds:

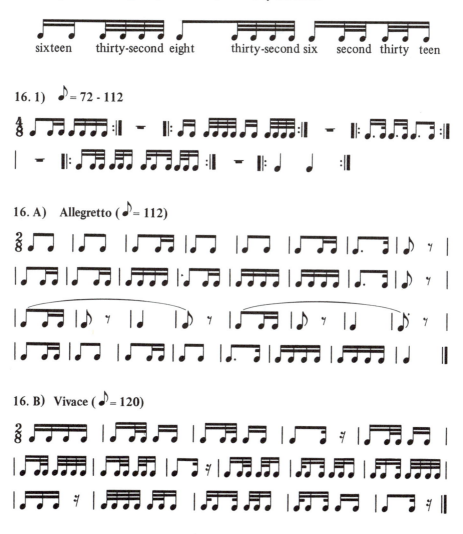

16. C)   Presto (♪ = 184)

16. D)   Largo (♪ = 60)

16. E)   Allegretto (♪ = 92)

16. F)   Allegro moderato (♪ = 108)

16. 2)   ♪ = 44 - 76

16. G)   Allegretto (♪ = 112)

16. H)   Allegro (♪ = 120)

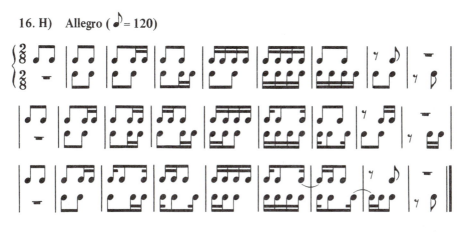

16. I)   Adagio (♪ = 56)

16. J)   Allegretto (♪ = 96)

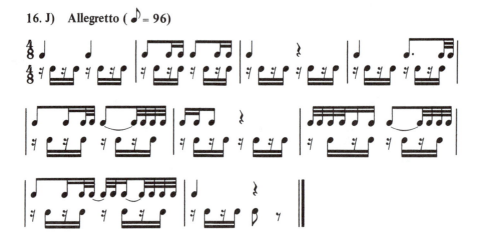

17. DOTTED-EIGHTH-NOTE BEAT

Again, the problem here is one of reading. In order to read six-sixteen or nine-sixteen meter, we must be able to see a dotted quarter as two beats and ♫ as a whole beat.

17. 1)   ♪. = 44 - 76

17. A)   Allegretto (♪. = 72)

17. B)   Adagio (♪. = 48)

17. C)   Allegro moderato (♪. = 72)

17. D)   Allegretto (♪. = 63)

17. E)   Andante con moto (♪. = 52)

17. F)   Allegro ma non troppo (♪. = 88)

17. 2)   ♪. = 40 - 60

17. G)   Allegro (♪. = 92)

17. H)   Vivo (♪. = 138)

17. I)   Andante (♪. = 56)

18. SMALL SUBDIVISIONS

We encountered thirty-second-notes in two-eight and three-eight meter; we encountered division of the beat into eight when sixteenth-notes appeared in a half-note beat. Only sixty-fourth-notes, dividing the quarter-note beat into sixteen, are new here. Such small subdivisions occur in slow tempi and are often ornamental; they should be sung lightly and easily.

As elsewhere, the more complicated single-beat patterns should be learned before whole measures of the exercises are attempted. Tapping steady eighths or sixteenth-notes will help in learning the more complicated patterns.

18. 1) ♩ = 40 - 60

18. A)   Largo (♩ = 48)

18. B)   Adagio (♩ = 52)

18. C)   Largo (♩ = 48)

18. 2) ♪ = 44 - 60

18. D)   Lento (♪ = 60)

18. 3)   ♪ = 80 - 108

18. E)   Lento (♩. = 40)

18. F)   Andante (♩. = 36, ♪ = 108)

18. 4) ♩ = 40 - 52

18. G)   Andante (♩ = 44)

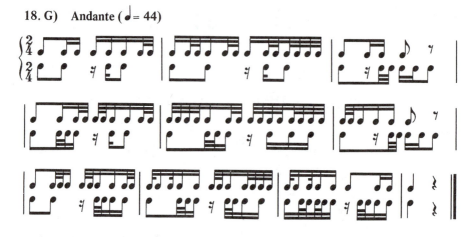

18. H)   Largo (♩ = 48)

18. I)   Adagio (♪ = 92)

19. CHANGING SIMPLE METER

When changing meter, we must know what the new meter is well before beginning the measure. Even though it may seem especially difficult, conducting is particularly helpful in these studies because it forces us to be aware of the meter before we make the gesture of the downbeat, since that gesture is different in different meters. Good preparation for these studies is conducting the measures and simply counting the beats aloud, so we become familiar with the succession of meters before tackling the actual rhythms.

19. 1) ♩ = 100 - 176

19. A) Vivace (♩ = 176)

19. B) Allegro (♩ = 160)

19. C) Presto (♩ = 192)

19. D) Allegretto (♩ = 80)

19. E)   Allegro (♩ = 100)

19. F)   Allegro ma non troppo (♩ = 88)

19. 2)   ♩ = 72 - 144

19. G)   Allegro (♩ = 132)

19. H)   Vivo (♩ = 144)

19. 3)   ♩ = 60 - 96

19. I)   Andante (♩ = 66)

20. CHANGING COMPOUND METER

As in changing simple meter, it is helpful to count the beats while conducting the meter before tackling the actual rhythm of each study. Conducting while performing the studies helps us feel physically the succession of meters.

20. 1)   ♩. = 56 - 76

20. A)   Presto (♩. = 120)

20. B)   Vivo (♩. = 132)

20. C)   Allegro (♩. = 92)

20. D)   Andante (♩. = 60)

20. E)   Adagio (♩. = 56)

20. F)   Allegretto (♩. = 66)

20. 2)   ♩. = 44 - 60

20. G)   Allegretto (♩. = 80)

20. H)   Andante (♩. = 52)

20. I)   Allegretto (♩. = 60)

20. J)   Andante (♩. = 54)

21. CHANGING BETWEEN SIMPLE AND COMPOUND METER WITH THE DIVISION CONSTANT

When changing between simple and compound meter, as between two-four and six-eight time, there is normally an equivalence either between the beats or between the divisions of the beats. In this chapter, the division of the beat remains constant: When moving between two-four and six-eight, the eighth-note remains the same. This means that the beat is longer in compound meter, where it has three eighths instead of two, and so the tempo is slower. Moving from six-eight to two-four, the tempo speeds up because the beat is shorter. If the eighth-note is constant at 216, for example, the tempo in two-four or three-four will be half of that, ♩=108, while the tempo in six-eight or nine-eight will be a third of 216, or ♩.=72. The tempi of the three note-values are given only for the first exercise and study; for the rest, those not given can be derived from those that are.

Tapping the eighth-note throughout a study, or using the metronome at the speed of the eighth, helps ensure the steadiness of the eighth as the meter changes.   Studies that alternate between six-eight and three-four can also be practiced with the metronome at the value of the quarter (making a cross-rhythm with the six-eight measures) and at the value of the dotted quarter (making a cross-rhythm with the two-four measures). Similarly, studies alternating between six-eight and two-four can be practiced with the metronome set at the speed of the quarter-note; those alternating between nine-eight and three-four can be practiced with the metronome at the speed of the dotted quarter.

Counting the number of eighths on a beat, while conducting the meter, is good preparation for the studies:

Normally, when meter changes between simple and compound, the equivalence – ♪ = ♪ or ♩. = ♩ – must be shown at the point of the change. This has not been done in these studies because the eighth is always constant.

21. 1) ♪ constant, ♩ = 72 - 120, ♩. = 48 - 80, ♪ = 144 - 240

21. A)   Allegretto, ♪ constant (♩. = 80, ♪ = 240, ♩ = 120)

21. B)   Presto, ♪ constant (♩=144)

21. C)   Allegretto, ♪ constant (♩·= 56)

21. D)   Andante con moto, ♪ constant (♪= 144)

21. E)   Allegretto, ♪ constant (♩ = 80)

21. F)   Allegro, ♪ constant (♩. = 72)

21. 2)   ♪ constant, ♩. = 56 - 112, ♩ = 84 - 168, ♪ = 168 - 336

21. G)   Presto, ♪ constant (♩. = 96, ♩ = 144)

21. H)   Andante, ♪ constant (♩ = 63)

21. I)   Vivace, ♪ constant (♩. = 80)

21. J)   Allegro, ♪ constant (♩ = 138)

22. CHANGING BETWEEN SIMPLE AND COMPOUND METER WITH THE BEAT CONSTANT

In this chapter, when moving between simple and compound meter, the beat remains constant: the dotted quarter in compound meter equals the quarter-note in simple meter. For example, the eighth-note in six-eight is only two-thirds as long as the eighth-note in two-four. The change is the same as that between duplet and triplet eighths in simple time or between eighths and dotted eighths in compound time. This is shown in Exercise 22.1, where the second and fourth segments, with changes of meter, sound the same as the first and third segments, where only the division of the beat changes.

Because they have the same number of beats, six-eight and two-four measures have the same length, as do three-four and nine-eight measures. However, a six-eight measure, with two beats, will be shorter than a three-four measure, even though measures in the two meters may have identical successions of note-values, as in Study 22.J.

22. 1)   ⅜ ♩. = ²₄ ♩ = 44 - 72

22. A)   Allegro, $\frac{6}{8}$ ♩. = $\frac{2}{4}$ ♩ (= 104)

22. B)   Allegretto, $\frac{6}{8}$ ♩. = $\frac{2}{4}$ ♩ (= 72)

22. C)   Andante, $\frac{9}{8}$ ♩. = $\frac{3}{4}$ ♩ (= 60)

22. D)   Adagio, $\frac{9}{8}$ ♩. = $\frac{3}{4}$ ♩ (= 52)

22. E)   Allegro ma non troppo, $\frac{6}{8}$ ♩. = $\frac{9}{8}$ ♩. = $\frac{3}{4}$ ♩ (= 92)

22. F)   Allegretto, $\frac{9}{8}$ ♩. = $\frac{6}{8}$ ♩. = $\frac{3}{4}$ ♩ = $\frac{2}{4}$ ♩ (= 72)

22. 2) $\frac{6}{8}$ ♩. = $\frac{2}{4}$ ♩ = 52 - 72

22. G)   Andante, $\frac{9}{8}$ ♩. = $\frac{3}{4}$ ♩ (= 58)

22. H)   Adagio, $\frac{3}{4}$ ♩ = $\frac{6}{8}$ ♩. (= 52)

22. I)   Allegro, $\frac{3}{4}$ ♩ = $\frac{9}{8}$ ♩. = $\frac{2}{4}$ ♩ (= 112)

22. J)   Allegretto, $\frac{3}{4}$ ♩ = $\frac{6}{8}$ ♩. (= 69)

23. THREE NOTES IN TWO BEATS; TWO NOTES IN THREE BEATS

The proportions involved in putting two equal notes in three beats and three equal notes in two beats are familiar from earlier chapters. In Chapter 10, two dotted eighths were put in a dotted-quarter beat; in Chapter 12, triplets were put in beats normally divided into duplets; in Chapter 13, two notes were put against three notes in a beat. What is new here is changing the division of the measure rather than the division of the beat.

In moving from normal quarter-notes to triplet quarters, it is helpful to think triplet eighths ahead of time, since two triplet eighths equal a triplet quarter:

Thinking [♪♪♪ ♪♪♪] facilitates performing [♪♪♪ ♪♪♪] = [♩ ♩ ♩].

Conducting helps steady the beat against which the cross–rhythms play. When we perform triplet quarter-notes, we must move quickly to the second note; when a triplet is performed unevenly, almost always it is the first note that is too long.

The hemiola pattern is most often three half-notes in the time of two three-

four measures: $\frac{3}{4}$ ♩ ♩ | ♩ ♩ .   Study 23.F presents the hemiola rhythm

in patterns familiar from the third movement of Schumann's Piano Concerto where, with one beat to a three-four measure, we hear the three half-notes against two downbeats.

23. 1) $\frac{6}{8}$ ♩. = $\frac{2}{4}$ ♩ = 63 - 108

23. A)   Allegro moderato (♩. = 72)

23. B)   Presto (♩ = 126)

23. C)   Andante con moto (♩ = 80)

23. D)   Allegro (♩ = 116)

23. E)   Allegro moderato (♩ = 104)

23. 2)   ♩. = 60 - 120 (Conduct one to a measure.)

23. F)   Vivace (♩. = 72) (Conduct one to a measure.)

23. 3)   ♩ = 88 - 176

23. G)   Allegretto (♩ = 112)

23. H)   Allegro (♩ = 160)

23. 4)   ⁶₈ ♩· = ²₄ ♩ = 60 - 116

23. I)   Allegro (♩· = 100)

23. J)   Allegretto (♩. = 72)

23. K)   Allegretto (♩ = 80)

23. L)   Allegro (♩ = 120)

24. FOUR AGAINST THREE

As twelve is the common denominator of four and three, the rhythm of four sixteenth-notes against triplet eighths is measured in twelfths of a beat. The sixteenths are attacked on the first, fourth, seventh, and tenth parts of the beat, and the triplets are attacked on the first, fifth, and ninth parts of the beat. As with the performance of two against three, we may be aided by verbal phrases that we speak naturally in these rhythms:

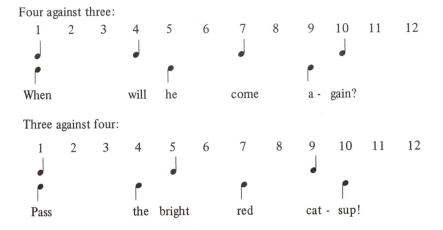

It is important to practice the cross-rhythms slowly so as to ensure accuracy and quickly so as to arrive at the point where we hear not just the composite rhythm but each part independently. Finally, we should feel that we are performing two conflicting patterns at the same time and that, although they fit together correctly, neither one is based on the other: We don't think sixteenths and fit a triplet against them, or vice versa; we simply sing four sixteenths and clap three, or sing a triplet and clap sixteenth notes, at the same time. We think two different thoughts simultaneously.

24. 1)   ♩ = 40 - 72

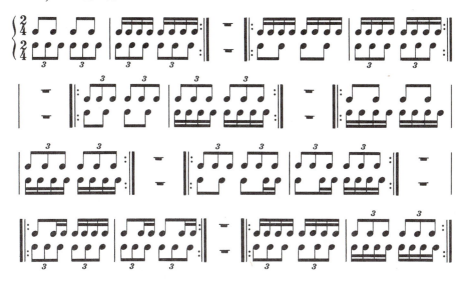

24. A)   Andante ($\frac{3}{4}$ ♩ = $\frac{9}{8}$ ♩. = 60)

24. B)   Allegretto (♩ = 66)

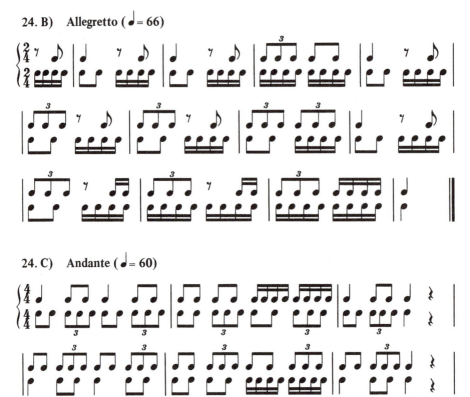

24. C)   Andante (♩ = 60)

24. D)   Allegretto ($\frac{2}{4}$ ♩ = $\frac{6}{8}$ ♩. = 72)

24. E)   Adagio (♩ = 52)

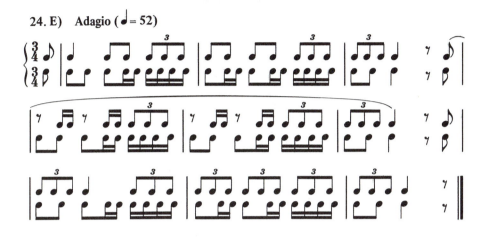

24. F)   Adagio (♩ = 50)

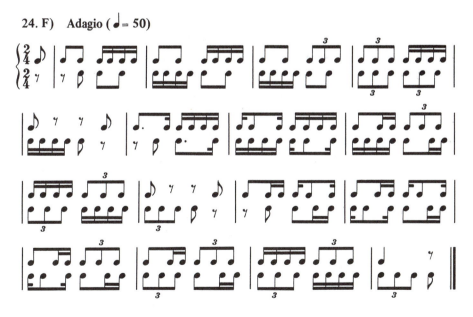

25. FOUR NOTES IN THREE BEATS;
THREE NOTES IN FOUR BEATS

Singing four even notes in the time of three beats is performing four against three at the level of the measure. Each of the four quadruplet quarters in a three-four measure is three-quarters of a beat long; thus, the pattern can be notated as the equivalent of four dotted eighths, but it is more commonly notated as a quadruplet:

Singing three even notes in the time of four beats is most easily done in twelve-eight time, where each of the three notes has the value of four eighth-notes, or a half-note. When the meter is four-four, a background of triplet eighths should be imagined:

Tapping the note that is the common denominator (the sixteenth for four notes in three beats, the triplet eighth for three notes in four beats) will help us learn to hear the proportions correctly. As with other cross-rhythms, performance at a fast tempo is a process different from slow performance, so the patterns should be practiced both slowly and quickly.

25. 1)   ♩ = 60 - 120 (Measure 4 is equivalent to measure 3.)

25. A)   Adagio (♩ = 63)

25. B)   Allegro (♩ = 132)

25. C)   Moderato (♩ = 88)

25. 2) $\frac{12}{8}$ ♩. = $\frac{4}{4}$ ♩ = 60 - 120 (Measure 4 is equivalent to measure 3.)

25. D)   Allegro (♩. = 112)

25. E)   Allegro (♩ = 126)

25. F)   Allegretto (♩· = 88)

25. 3)   ♩ = 56 - 88

25. G)   Allegretto (♩ = 72)

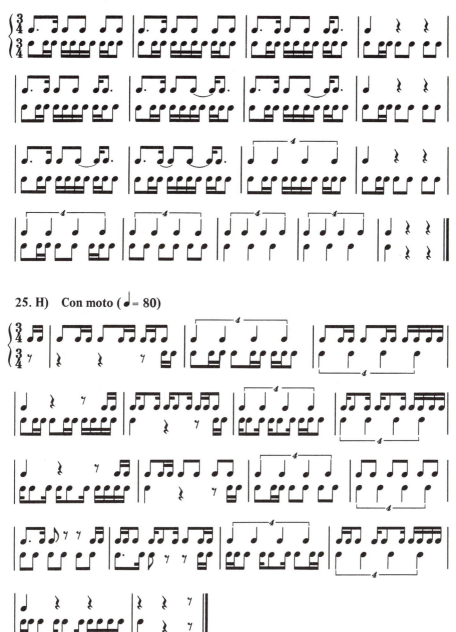

25. H)   Con moto (♩ = 80)

25. 4) $^{12}_{8}$ $\downarrow\cdot = ^4_4$ $\downarrow = 50 - 80$

25. I)   Allegretto ($\downarrow\cdot = 96$)

25. J)   Allegretto ($\downarrow = 100$)

26. QUINTUPLETS

Counting the notes helps us put the five notes of a quintuplet onto a beat, especially in a context of other divisions of the beat:

To sing five equal notes in two beats, we need to think the quintuplet beat:

The common denominator of five and two is ten, but to perform five against two, we need think only of the second note of the duplet dividing the third note of the quintuplet:

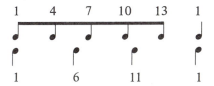

The common denominator of five and three is fifteen, so the second note of the triplet sounds a fifteenth of a beat before the third note of the quintuplet, and the third note of the triplet sounds a fifteenth of a beat after the fourth note of the quintuplet:

As with other cross-rhythms, learning must begin with careful counting, proceed to slow performance where the subdivisions can be imagined and the composite rhythm heard to be accurate, and arrive at the point where the two patterns are performed and heard simultaneously and independently.

26. 1) 𝅗𝅥 = 48 - 76

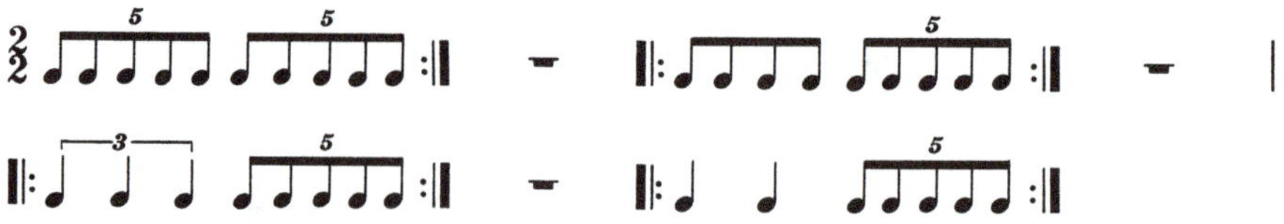

26. A) Larghetto (𝅗𝅥 = 52)

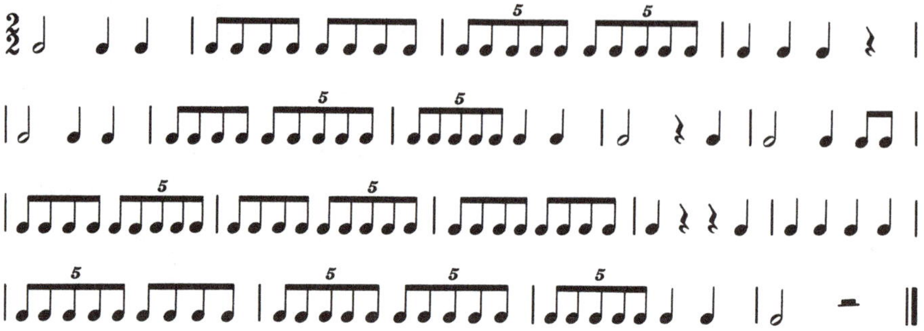

26. B) Andante (𝅗𝅥 = 76)

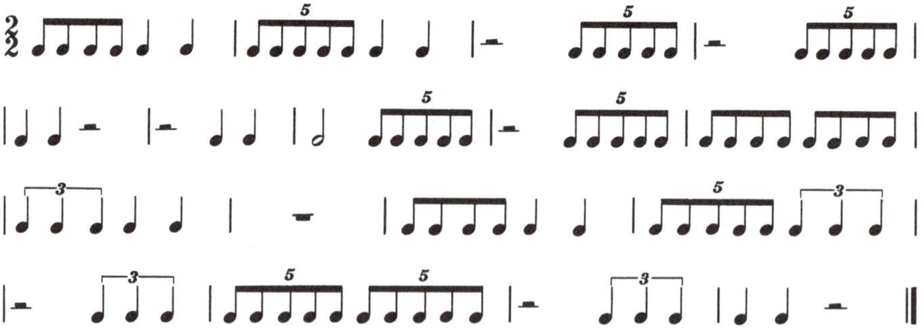

26. 2) ♩= 48 - 76

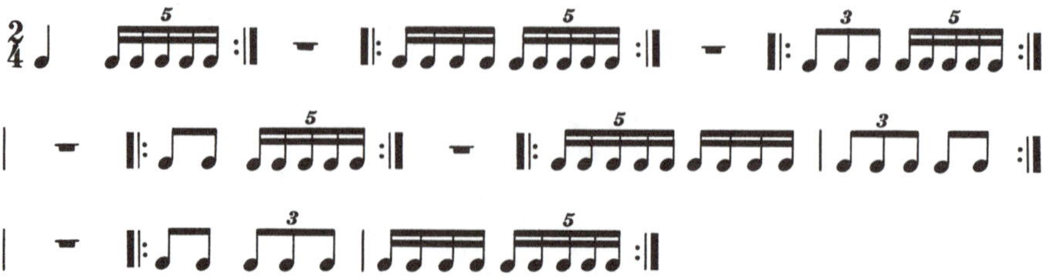

26. C)   Andante (♩ = 63)

26. D)   Allegro (♩ = 80)

26. 3)   ♩ = 54 ÷ 80

26. E)   Allegretto (♩ = 76)

26. F)   Andante (♩ = 60)

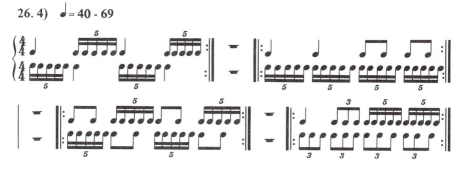

26. 4)   ♩ = 40 - 69

26. G)   Adagio (♩ = 54)

26. H)   Allegretto (♩ = 63)

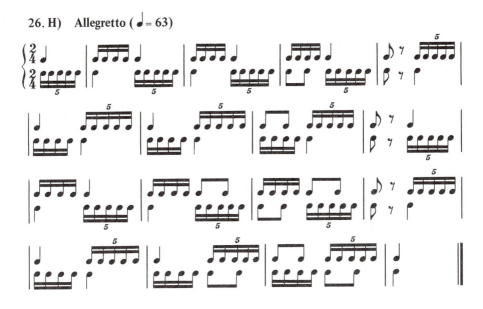

26. I)   Moderato (♩ = 72)

26. J)   Andante (♩ = 60)

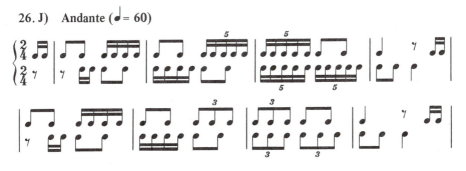

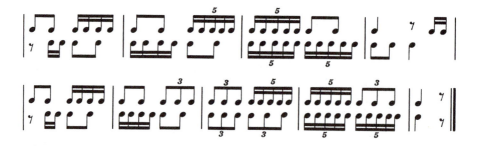

27. FIVE-EIGHT METER

While slow quintuple meter may be understood as having five beats in a measure, five-eight meter is most often not quintuple meter, but duple meter with two unequal beats, one a quarter-note and the other a dotted quarter. For example, when the tempo of the eighth-note is 240, the quarter-note is 120, the dotted quarter is 80, and these slower values are the effective tempo. Most of these studies should be understood, and conducted, with two unequal beats in a measure.

It is important to conduct the larger unequal beats, not their eighth-note divisions, in order to feel the beats physically. After years of striving to keep the beat steady, unequal beats will seem strange. The other hand or a foot may tap the underlying quick pulse to keep the beats in their proper ratios, and the metronome may help for this purpose.

The grouping of the eighths into 2 + 3 or 3 + 2 is shown in several ways. Where the grouping is consistent, the meter signature will indicate it, as in the first two studies. Beams will usually make the beats visible: ♩ ♪♫ is 3 + 2, whereas ♩ ♫♩ is 2 + 3. As quarter-eighth is a more normal pattern than eighth-quarter, an eighth between two quarters may be assumed to belong to the first beat — ♩ ♪♩ is 3 + 2 — if there is no contrary indication. Where there might otherwise be ambiguity, the beginning of a beat will be marked with an accent, or brackets will group the notes on a beat.

27. 1)   ♪ = 144 - 208

27. A)   Allegro (in 2) (♪ = 240, ♩ = 120, ♩. = 80, ♩. ♩ = 48)

27. B)   Vivace (♪ = 330)

27. C)   Allegro (♪ = 280)

27. D)   Adagio (♪ = 80)

27. E)   Allegro (♪ = 192)

27. F)   Andante (♪ = 160)

27. 2)   ♪ = 100 - 144

27. G)   Presto (♪ = 264)

27. H)   Presto (♪ = 300)

27. I)   Andante (♪ = 108)

27. J)   Allegretto (♪ = 132)

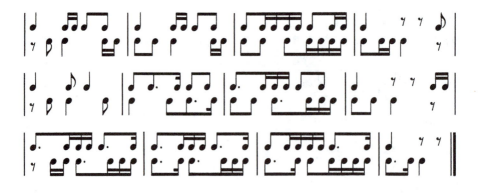

28. MORE METERS WITH UNEQUAL BEATS

The meters in this chapter combine quarter-note and dotted-quarter beats just as five-eight meter does. Here, in each case, the meter signature makes the sequence of beats explicit. For example, $^{2+2+3}_{\quad 8}$ is $\frac{7}{8}$, but with three beats, of which the first two are quarters and the third is a dotted quarter. Conducting again helps us become comfortable with patterns of unequal beats, and tapping the underlying eighth-note helps us keep the proportions accurate.

28. 1)   ♪ = 160 - 288

28. A)   Allegro (♩ = 138, ♩. = 92)

28. 2)   ♪ = 160 - 208

28. B)   Allegretto (♪ = 192)

28. 3)   ♪ = 160 - 208

28. C)   Allegro (♪ = 208)

28. 4)   ♪ = 160 - 224

28. D)   Andante con moto, in 4 (♪ = 160)

28. E)   Vivo (♩ = 162, ♩. = 108)

28. F)   Andante (♩ = 80, ♩. = 53)

28. 5)   ♪ = 120 - 200

28. G)   Allegretto (♪ = 184)

28. 6)   ♪ = 144 - 224

28. H)   Allegro (♪ = 216)

28. 7) ♪ = 120 - 184

28. I)   Andante (♪ = 144)

28. J)   Grazioso (♪ = 116)

29. CHANGING METERS WITH UNEQUAL BEATS

The best preparation for these studies is counting the eighths on each beat aloud while conducting the larger beats, thereby becoming familiar with the metrical patterns before attempting the actual rhythms. Thus, while conducting seven-eight in three and five-eight in two, we would count:

$$\text{[musical notation]}$$

.1 2   1 2   3 1 2   1 2   1 2 3

Tapping the eighth while singing the rhythm is especially important for studies such as 29.B where there are many notes longer than eighths.

Studies 29.F and 29.I, and the exercises that immediately precede them, include three-sixteen and five-sixteen measures. The sixteenth-note rather than the eighth-note is the basic division of the beat, and beats are eighths and dotted eighths. In these studies, therefore, two-eight and five-sixteen measures have two beats, three-eight and seven-sixteen measures have three beats, and a three-sixteen measure is a single dotted-eighth beat.

29. 1)   ♪ = 176 - 240

$$\text{[musical notation]}$$

29. A)   Allegretto,   ♪ constant (♪ = 176)

$$\text{[musical notation]}$$

29. B)   Allegro (♪ = 208)

29. C)   Vivace (♩. = 96, ♩ = 144)

29. D)   Allegro (♩. = 72, ♩ = 108)

29. E)   Allegro ma non troppo, ♪ constant (♪= 224)

29. 2)   ♪ constant, ♪ = 176 - 300

29. F)   Presto, ♪ constant (♪= 144)

29. 3)   ♪ = 152 - 208

29. G)   Allegretto (♪ = 208)

29. 4)   ♪ = 120 - 168

29. H)   Andante con moto (♪ = 168)

29. 5) ♪ constant, ♪ = 184 - 240

29. I)   Vivace, ♪ constant (♪ = 240)

29. 6) ♪ = 120 - 184

29. J)   Grazioso ($\flat$ = 160)

30. TEMPO MODULATION

In these studies, tempo is changed in two different ways. The same note-value may have the same speed in meters with different numbers of that value on the beat, so the beat becomes longer or shorter. For example, as we saw in Chapter 21, when the eighth-note stays the same in moving from simple to compound meter, the beat becomes longer and the tempo slower. Alternatively, different note-values may be given the same speed. For example, when a quintuplet sixteenth is equated to a preceding normal sixteenth, the beat, now consisting of five sixteenths, becomes longer. The terms *metric modulation* and *tempo modulation* have both been applied to these procedures for changing tempo, but the latter is more accurate.

Each of the preparatory exercises in this chapter should be performed three times in succession, beginning at the first of the indicated tempi; we will then arrive at the other tempi during the course of the exercise. In the first exercise, 30.1a, if the quarter-note is initially 162, the eighth is 324, and the dotted quarter is 108; at the return to two-four, the 108 beat is kept; beginning again at 108, the eighth is 216, and the dotted quarter is 72; the third time, then, we begin at 72, the eighth is 144, and the dotted quarter is 48, which is the speed of the final quarter-note.

It will be helpful to figure out the tempo at each point during the exercises and studies where values are marked as equivalent. As always, conducting will make us physically aware of the changes of tempo.

30. 1a) ♩ = 162, 108, 72, 48

30. 1b) ♩ = 48, 72, 108, 162

30. 1c) ♩ = 48, 72, 108, 162

30. A)   Beginning Vivace (♩ = 144, 96, 64)

30. B)   Beginning Andante (beat = 48, 72, 108)

30. 2a) ♩ = 54, 72, 96, 128

30. 2b) ♩ = 128, 96, 72, 54

30. C)   Beginning Andante (beat = 63, 84, 112, 84, 63)

30. D)   Beginning Allegro (♩ = 128, 96, 72, 96, 128)

30. 3a) ♩ = 48, 60, 75, ca. 94

30. 3b) ♩ = 100, 80, 64, ca. 51

30. E)   Beginning Moderato (♩ = 64, 80, 100, 80, 64)

30. 4) ♩ = 84, 70, ca. 58, ca. 49

30. F)   Beginning Andante (beat = 60, 72, 90, 120, 90, 72, 60)

30. G)   Beginning Lento (♩. = 40, 60, 90)

30. H)   Beginning Adagio (beat = 50, 60, 72)

30. 5)   ♩ = 72, 96, 128, ca. 171

30. I)   **Beginning Andante** (♩ = 63, 84, 112)

30. 6)   ♩ = 160, 120, 90, 67.5

30. J)   **Beginning Allegro** (♩ = 120, 90)